D1461466

RUTH BIDGOOD

Cinnamon Press
:: small miracles from distinctive voices ::

Published by Cinnamon Press
Meirion House
Tanygrisiau
Blaenau Ffestiniog
Gwynedd, LL41 3SU
www.cinnamonpress.com

The right of Ruth Bidgood to be identified as author of this work has been asserted by her in accordance with the Copyright, Designs and Patent Act, 1988. Copyright © 2019 Ruth Bidgood. ISBN: 978-1-78864-084-8
British Library Cataloguing in Publication Data. A CIP record for this book can be obtained from the British Library.
Designed and typeset in Palatino by Cinnamon Press.
Cover design by Adam Craig. Printed in Poland
Cinnamon Press is represented in the UK by Inpress Ltd and in Wales by the Welsh Books Council

Acknowledgements

Some of these poems appeared in the following journals to which acknowledgment is made: Envoi, London Grip, Poetry Salzburg Review, Scintilla. An early version of 'Shut Door' appeared in the *Wallich Clifford Anthology*.

Contents

Lights

Lights

for Jonah

Dusk, and lights coming on,
that's what he would paint—
a picture for children—not, he said,
photographic, not quite this valley
we were wandering up.

He'd asked me to take him there,
wanted to see how spurs of hill
folded one on another, how
nearby farms could shout
with loud light, be met
with answers subtle and faint
from lost houses so far upstream
his picture would hint, not state.

He wanted the children to learn
the mingling of here and now
with gone, to wonder what 'gone'
can mean in a valley like this,
among hills that hide and show,
lift up and tuck away, where
the hardly-remembered
shines like today. Now he too
is gone.

       I have his painted sketch
for the children's picture. To me
it seems to spell out lost and now,
as truly as on the day we walked
and he saw imagined lights,
the furthest far and high, so small,
its tiny calling voice so real.

Music Upstream

I remember a young musician
living here once,
the last house up the valley.
Often, three girls on ponies
would climb through the woods,
past the loud waterfall,
up onto the hill, to visit him.

Amiable, gently detached, he made tea
and went on tuning his piano.
For the girls, the remote house,
the cool comely host,
were enigma, romance.

Yet that was inherent
in the place too—the sense
of miles of rising land beyond,
cleft by a valley that climbed
from softness into wild—
at its head a cairned mountain.

In after-years, could memory disentangle
the man from his house, from the land,
his music from acre on acre of beauty
stretching away below, or, felt more than seen,
the climbing miles along the young stream's
dwindling measures, and over dark moors
to a darker mountain?

Perhaps here there was a unity,
something made by the heart's
diverse songs, something those girls would keep
without understanding anything more
than when they sat on the sunny grass
near their grazing ponies,
half listening to the tuned piano,
turning in their young hands
mugs of welcoming tea.

Lugg Meadows

The trees are rushing, rushing—
they tear and leap. Their affinity
is with the scudding clouds,
white, grey, driven; little to do,
it seems ,with clumpy grass,
red-banked cleft where the Lugg
moves gently, unseen.

        The men earth us,
one hunched on a plodding horse, the other
on foot, slow alongside; even
the dogs pausing, taking no note
of soft stir of sheep on the further bank.

How complete it all is! The painter
understands contradiction
at the heart of fullness,
and finds it here.

Flowers for Easter

I set a pot of flowers
on the stone shelf under her name, and find
others already there-from a stranger,
who thought this grave forgotten?
                Trimming
encroaching grass, I'm conscious
of the valley stretching behind me,
over the crumbling graveyard wall,
far into hills.
            There she would ride
on borrowed ponies, in her happy years.
Today's jumble of fancy and memory
brings a sense of the teenager, laughing,
tearing down-valley on her palomino,
triumphing, joined with the land's grandeur.
Ears just catch the muted pounding
of hooves on turf, the far-away beat
timelessly thudding through the ground.

The Huntsman

I still see them running, slipping
on the loose stones of Caban Coch,
above Coedmynach, down to Glanelan
for the waiting horses, and away.

One day in the yard
the huntsman lounged by the wall,
the hounds all over him.
He was fondling them, and looking at her.
'I wish to God they were mine,' he said,
and she, 'They could be!'

When she was a child, a scrawny, sandy thing,
I was steward to her father.
She would beg a ride on my saddle;
I held her safe. After her father died
it was me she would ride with, if anyone.
Many a time I had only half an eye
for tenants' fences, or the stock on Gelynen,
when she seemed over-long away, alone
on Cwmdauddwr hills.

His rough hand slides gentle
down the hound's back; the young girl
smiles at him.
        The child
is lifted to the saddle, turns in my arms,
smiling up at me.
        Away they go,
scrambling hand in hand along the Caban,
her sandy hair blown across her face.

'Take me with you!' calls the child,
and I lift her, hold her.

They are off along the hill, going away.
She almost forgets to wave.

The child swings down from my arms,
waves as she runs away.

Viewpoint

The village is silent today, looks empty,
as if the last humans have died,
and all they built will soon be gone.
The hills have come into their own.

Yet even they will change, become a plain,
or ocean shore. Heights I see as shelter
will burn with the rest of Earth one day,
our home be unremembered—except perhaps
by some sentient being on a living world
who predicts, observes, records this tiny event
unimaginable light-years away.

I look again, seeing now
the village pausing, sleepily enclosed,
soon to wake, ripple, find voices to assert
the living, ordinary, diverse.
Meaning's not lost but changed,
vulnerability an added beauty worn
by gentle impermanent hills.

Barn

From the crest of the road, the view ahead,
and sweeping away to the right,
was wide and gentle,
with its velvety valley, treeless, riverless,
its undulations of hill.

To the left was another valley, where (I knew)
woods climbed a rocky slope,
and a river ran. But sight was blocked
by a crumbling barn, once perhaps
of workmanlike dignity, now a shambles,
a derelict obstruction. I wished it gone,
with its glimpse of murky interior
cluttered with fallen beams,
planks every which way, obscure
sullied objects to trip the step.

I was away for a year. Then one day, climbing again,
I found the barn demolished, carted away.
And yet where was the delight
surely I should have known?

Trudging home, puzzled, dissatisfied,
I wondered if what was lacking might be
a link I'd never valued, with things
human, ordinary — work, laughter,
sweat, weariness, air pungent,
or heavy with the sweetness of hay,
in cavernous dimness; and when men left,
creak of a sagging door.

Moriah Chapel

Door-paint flaking, tiles lying splintered
by peeling walls, graveyard dunged and trodden
by straying sheep, the chapel seems
part of the landscape, not so clearly
related to man's reach for the divine.
There used to be customary plod
to accepted observance, and once in a while
flare of wildness when a preacher had the Word.

It's not so long since the tale was told,
and understood, of five men sitting
in the vestry (in their day neat and scoured),
one urging his fellows to join him in prayer,
start a revival—a thing possible, needing
only faith and perseverance.

They prayed, and prayed again,
each time disappointed, yet knowing
stronger resolve would bring
the thrilling fire. At last it came.
Excited praying, singing, abasement,
glorying, swept outwards for miles,
had its year of triumph.

The broken chapel, belonging in its decay
to the life of river and hill, has not,
perhaps, lost that fervour
but holds it as part of a story—
beginning far distant, end unknown.

The Forcing

It was a valley where some still alive
remembered hunger. Now to have
too much was joy, wonder,
one's gift to the honoured guest.
was 'the forcing' —never taking 'no',
however honestly that guest begged
respite, however bloat and twinges
were ruining his meal, still
the extra slice slid onto his plate,
sharply watched till its disappearance
left an empty patch to be promptly,
cruelly filled.

       The loud 'No!'
of one minister could not be ignored.
'But what would you like, dear Mr Jones,
what can I give you next?'
The response was ruefully remembered
for years—'Peace, woman, peace!'
To have failed with the forcing,
failed with the greatest skill
of the hostess! So many vast meals
were to come, so many times
when the extra slice
sneaked onto the plate—yet some pride
is never mended, some ignominy
never forgotten.

Question and Answer

What, I asked, was for him
the meaning of 'belief'?
How did it come about,
this total acceptance
of the unprovable—beyond
all argument, fact
incontrovertible?
           Smiling, he said
belief was where all pattern started;
for him it was the essential
shape of truth, the birth-pang
thrusting beauty into the world.

I was left pondering propositions
with meaning other than the known,
significance contradictory, dark,
and yet an avatar of something
I could almost take for light.

Not Loving the Sea

Had the sea sentience to meet mine,
I might apologise for my lack of love.
'Grand,' I can say, 'supremely beautiful,' never
'How I love it!' I know it's fear that inhibits—
of depths, that horrify and draw me down,
of sick pitching and yawing, lives swept away
by overweening tempestuousness. I can't forget
that under the glinting sway of that surface
splendour, there plunges a stifling impermeable
blackness, negation of any life I could welcome;
a harbour, surely, for the monstrous only; and the roots
of mountain peaks whose terror, for me,
is that only the savagery of earthquake allows
them to rise into air and sun. Never
can I forget the unspeakable dark,
which is the womb of islands.

Resettling the Abos

Abos rounded up
from their huge red wilderness,
neatly slotted into a reserve.

Roofs over heads now.
No more naked freedom.
No more finger-drilling
down through aridity
for succulent grubs.
Pudgy women, buttoned
into drooping dresses,
plod from their supermarket,
shopping-bags crammed with fish fingers,
oven chips, boxes of tartlets.

Twice a year, day out —
bus trip (perfunctory link
with old life in the wild), all the way
to caves of the ancestors.
Pictures on rock-walls
each year less understood,
like ancient words
an aged elder recites.
One year the bus will stop coming,
hardly regretted.

Last shot in the film
clings to my mind —
a white carrier-bag,
stuck on the fence,
whipped off by hot wind,
whirling away
over the vast red land —
further, further, tinier, white dot,
gone.

Shut Door

Furious again, his mother slams the door,
barring him even from her anger.
Tearless, he presses against cold wood,
his ragged jersey drooping.
One fat hand, open,
gently, desperately pats the door.
His head is bent on his crooked arm
in the ancient posture of grief,
adult, extreme.

Whatever pain waits
after however many years,
he will recognise it, unremembering.
Over and over the armoured man.
will suffer the child's defeat.
A woman looking into his eyes
will see with desolation, suddenly,
the spirit banished, gone out into the cold.

Book Cover

A novelist made a fiction
of his reality, of how they lived then;
grabbing, cheating,
love undervalued,
money their king.
An artist made a visual fiction
of how it looked then.
Out of our now,
we search for a then
to believe in. Is it in this
dunged street, horse-omnibus
looming out of the fog,
glare of lights through murk?
Those blurred black-swathed
figures by the lamp-post
have no words for us,
have no words for anyone.
What is their reality?
We ask and ask. It seems
we have to find a truth
not always cheapened,
not always dingy,
not always unwelcome.

One Light

Night. Where and when forgotten.
Seen from a shore, black buildings
climb on a starless sky. In one,
the tallest, shines the only light.
What most clearly I recall
is how that mattered, how much
I cared that it should shine—
but why is lost.
   For years
the memory is gone. Then suddenly
some chance, some random sighting,
something heard, read, can wake it—
and with it what I felt, still calling
out of the baffling past, still
dark as that distant night, still
strong as its only light.

Failure

Another's grief is a dangerous land.
I find no foothold on its crags—
whatever path I choose may prove
the clumsiness of my most cautious tread.
Silence or speech seems failure, stumble, fall,
and touch a brash intrusion. Is there
no entry-point to reach your dark domain?
Waiting outside its jagged boundaries
I dumbly make the offering of my pain.

Swing Doors

In winter dark, swing doors
creaked, swished, spun, swished, creaked,
swung shut. Their movement
was quick, repetitive, enclosing,
compulsive, as if you were caught
in their swinging, again and again,
as if the doors were always shutting,
as if you were shut in.

But it was not so—you had felt them
spin open, you had walked out
to a high place. Far below,
mile on mile, stretched away
an illimitable landscape, your home,
waiting, alive with lights.

Climbing at Noon

The hot hillside was a jungle
of shrogs and bushes.
We pushed our way
upwards, through invisible
scuttlings, flutterings, slidings.
Near the top, in amongst
scratchy shoots and tangles,
we sensed a sudden
sharper pouncing, an acting-out
of claustrophobic dark, an ending—
tiny, no doubt, yet with new
breathless effort we forced our way
up to the reassurance
of open hill, noonday sun.

Death of an Ant

So, brother ant, I have your death
in my hand. 'Quick acting,'
says the ant-powder. I hope that's true.
I have no instinctive dislike
of your small glossy frame,
your purposeful scuttling.
I can hardly call you
an undesirable alien. I'm aware
of much we could learn
from you and yours—your worthy
social life, its organised
complexity, deep dedication
to the common good, endless
hard work. Perhaps if you came
with just a small band, we could
co-exist. But there's the rub.
Below these tiles, with their chink,
their hardly visible exit
into my hall, your compatriots
pullulate… I maintain that this
is my house, my space, my land.
There are too many of you!
So, little brother, and all of your ilk,
farewell....

Losers

Glass emptying again, enjoy your fiction—
at least you know what should have been the truth.
Yearning achieved the golden transmutation
we wink at now, of all those well-tipped losers
that seen refracted in the beer spank in
first past the post, the way they should have done.

Like towering carnival giants, your fantasies
imply some pattern that life could not match.
Stepping from chatter and dazzle into night
and glancing back at you, I sigh, not smile.
My alchemy too has worked on tawdry fact;
behind your silly boasts the pain is mine.

Winter Moon

I remember showing a child, now man,
winter night's moon rising,
like this one tonight, huge and white
behind firs on the hill.
I gave him that moon to keep
with so many he'd not yet seen, moons
of sleepless longing, enigma, love.
This was a wild and staring presence;
he stared back, lips parted, but silent.
Tonight he is far away, among mountains.
Is moonlight part of that mystery?

The child's eyelids flickered, drooped.
I carried him into the warm.
I will never know if that moon
went on shining in skies of his mind;
am sure only that I received, to keep,
strange, unplanned, a winter gift.

Cinnamon Press
:: small miracles from distinctive voices ::